MAYBE IT WAS SO

Phoenix Poets

A SERIES EDITED BY ROBERT VON HALLBERG

REGINALD GIBBONS

# maybe
# it was so

THE UNIVERSITY OF CHICAGO PRESS
*Chicago and London*

REGINALD GIBBONS *is professor of English at Northwestern University and editor of* TriQuarterly *magazine. He is the author of three books of poetry,* Roofs Voices Roads, The Ruined Motel, *and* Saints. *He is also editor of* The Poet's Work *and co-editor of* From South Africa, *both published by the University of Chicago Press. "From a Paper Boat," the centerpiece of* Maybe It Was So, *won the 1991 John Masefield Memorial Award of the Poetry Society of America.*

The University of Chicago Press, Chicago 60637
The University of Chicago Press, Ltd., London
© 1991 by The University of Chicago
All rights reserved. Published 1991
Printed in the United States of America
00 99 98 97 96 95 94 93 92 91   5 4 3 2 1
ISBN 0-226-29055-7 (cloth)
ISBN 0-226-29056-5 (pbk.)

Library of Congress Cataloging-in-Publication Data

Gibbons, Reginald.
    Maybe it was so / Reginald Gibbons.
        p.   cm. — (Phoenix poets)
    I. Title.   II. Series.
  PS3557.I1392M3      1991
  811'.54—dc20                                91-14066
                                                CIP

*To C.M.S.*

Of seven roses on the rosebush
six belong to the wind.
But one is left, just one, and such
as only I have found.

Of seven times I call to you,
six, you're right to stay where you are.
But if only you would promise me
my seventh word will bring you here.

*after Brecht*

# Contents

# *Acknowledgments*

The author is grateful to the editors of the following magazines, where earlier versions of these poems have appeared:

*American Poetry Review* "Hide from Time," "Stars."
*The Atlantic* "The Affect of Elms," © 1990 by Reginald Gibbons, as first published in *The Atlantic,* June 1990.
*Boulevard* "Prospect of a Village in Devon."
*Chelsea* "Order of Battle."
*Chowder Review* "Lemon Trees."
*Ontario Review* "Hark."
*Poetry Durham* (England) "Piano (and Voice)," "A Rememberer."
*Poetry East* "From a Paper Boat," "One of César Vallejo's Human Poems," "Piano (and Voice)," "Retributions," "Poem." These poems appeared in *Poetry East #31.*
*Southwest Review* "Madrid."
*Webster Review* "Hungry Man Raids Supermarket."
*Wilderness* "Teacher."

one

# The Affect of Elms

Across the narrow street from the old hotel that now
houses human damage temporarily—
deranged, debilitated, but up and around in their odd
postures, taking their meds, or maybe trading them—

is the little park, once a neighboring mansion's side yard,
where beautiful huge old elm trees, long in that place,
stand in a close group over the mown green lawn
watered and well kept by the city, their shapes expressive:

the affect of elms is of struggle upward and survival,
of strength—despite past grief (the bowed languorous arches)
and torment (limbs in the last stopped attitude of writhing)—

while under them wander the deformed and tentative
persons, accompanied by voices, counting their footsteps,
exhaling the very breath the trees breathe in.

# Foreign Landscape

The dirt road crested at a flat, broad, open pass.
I stopped my car and got out.
Nowhere was another car in sight.

It had been desert, coming up the dusty switchbacks;
but below, on the new side,
there were steep green fields and a small flock of sheep
and, surrounding the prospect, low mountains.

Not far from the road a thread of chimney smoke
had tied a lonely summit inn to the deep sky
that was trying to withdraw above the blue forested slopes.

An old man and a boy were coming up the pitched path
with a great bucket of blueberries hanging from a pole
they carried between them on their shoulders.

Smiling, the boy came first, because he was shorter.
Then the old man, wearing old-fashioned gaiters.

Some other people, middle-aged and in city clothes,
appeared from the inn
and stood waiting for them at the top of the path,
reaching down to help lift the bucket up.
Distant sheepbells clanked
and the smooth fields were lowering beneath the old man and boy
who came rising into the air
sufficient, expected, and welcomed.

All of them walked to the inn,
one woman between the old man and boy,
her arms around their shoulders,
laughing.

# A Rememberer

It's a long list of those who had
less than nothing, who borrowed the money
for bread, who heard instead of a melody
the wind that whistled in under the door
in the bad hour between last light and night,
who must await neither friend nor kin
but force from strangers.

You'd read by the window a while longer.
Or give it up and wrap
your shoulders in a blanket, try to doze
in the dusty chair out of the drafts,
too tired to read.
Even half-sleeping, you'd go over
the memorized lines, not needing more than a whisper
to bring them back, with no one listening.
So I think of you
guarding the words inside
till they could find their road
to the world, or worlds could change.

In a small blue patch of specific chill
you sit—in time,
in that year, on that night, breathing
through stillness and cold
those words that could fill the lungs with air
or a ship with buoyancy over the deep,
that could fill memory with sweetness and grief,
hopelessness with hope,
with life, the stubborn mind.


*homage to Nadezhda Mandel'shtam*

# Koktobel. March 1920

*after Osip Mandel'shtam*

Two sisters—heaviness and tenderness—
have the same mien: as bees and wasps will ply
the same sweet languid rose. Men die, sands cool,
yesterday's sun in black is borne away.

Heavy honeycombs and tender webs!
Easier to heft a boulder than to speak
your name. One hope remains, like a distant gold
mirage: to throw time off my weary back.

The air that fills my lungs runs dark. And time's
ploughed under, roses rise from humble earth.
Whirling slowly, these heavy tender roses
plait a rose *tristesse, tendresse,* in a double wreath.

# Long-ago Yaupon

*after Eugenio Montale*

To rest—hidden, mid-afternoon, lightheaded and hot
in the only shade, the hollow center of a yaupon bush
when the glare needled in and no one would come,
to wonder about snakes, and listen to the wasps;

to watch red ants in a spread-out horde search
the cracked ground around you and underneath, so many
ant miles from the great city mounds you'd dynamited
with hoarded firecrackers, and then seen them rebuild;

to peer out of the bush at the low flat roof of the house,
its crushed white gypsum driving the sunlight back
while the locusts, we called them, raised their buzz
to fits of screeching across the bare acres;

and carefully crawling out with empty lunch sack and water jar
at last, self-exiled from the house but who cared,
to wonder with a boy's beginnings of sadness if all life and the
  work of men
wouldn't require hiding from the scald of light
under a bush topped with the throbbing paper nests of hornets.

# One of César Vallejo's Human Poems

**A** man goes by with a long loaf of bread on his human shoulder.
And after that I'm going to write about my double?

Another man sits down, scratches himself, nabs a louse in his
  armpit, smashes it.
What's the good of talking about psychoanalysis?

Another man has invaded my body with a stick in his hand.
So then, am I going to talk about Socrates later at the doctor's?

A cripple goes by with a boy, arm in arm.
And after that, I'm going to read André Breton?

Another man is shivering with the cold, he coughs, he spits blood.
Will it ever be right to refer to the Inner Me?

Another is looking for meat scraps and orange rinds in the mud.
How can I write about the Infinite after that?

A mason falls from a rooftop, he dies, and he does without lunch
  from now on.
And then I'm going to invent new tropes and metaphors?

A merchant cheats by one gram as he weighs out a customer's
   goods.
After that, talk about the fourth dimension?

A banker rigs his gold-balance.
Make a bawling scene at the theater?

One of the homeless sleeps with his foot behind his back.
And after that how can I talk to anyone about Picasso?

Someone is on the way to a burial, crying.
How is one supposed to be inducted into the Academy, later?

Someone's cleaning his rifle in the kitchen.
What's the good of talking about the beyond?

Someone goes by counting on his fingers.
How can I talk about the not-I without screaming?

# Hungry Man Raids Supermarket

The carts, half-filled and abandoned
for the moment, were strewn in the aisles
like some small riverside derailment
and a woman turned, looked
at me, cold streams fell
into the pit of my stomach,
she put her arm across
her son's shoulders—quickly—
and pulled him out of my path:
a boy whose face was hers
though in him the timidity was
less from fright than from
plainness and innocence, he didn't
smile upward at me like a suppliant
the way she did, from the shallows.
Already I had a sense
of having waded into myself
till I was up to my own hands
and the undertow pulling at me.
Her look made me recognize the deeps
into which I was stepping,
where the water came almost
to my mouth.

                    It wasn't the boy
I wanted, she didn't need
to shield him from me.
What story rising in her,
that she wouldn't tell perhaps
ever to anyone, led her
to such a fear for her child,
the premonitions rushing
at her all at once?

The water flowed by
under the overhanging trees,
mother and son stood beyond
the wrecked sleeping cars
in a little eddy to one side
and the boy looked up at her
for an answer but she had none,
it wasn't something she could explain to him—
her panic at seeing the man
who had stood near them, there,
at the place where they were
without husband or father,
then his stepping off into the hidden
suck-hole in the middle
(did he think he was going
to save some lives?) and not
coming up again . . .

And now the stranger was gone
into the cold pool of himself
the way a man will do,
where water closed over him
and the current spun down
into a point far from mothers and sons.

The danger was past,
they went on without him
down cold-lit store aisles again,
without what he would have told them
and without finding in themselves
what they would have had to tell.

# Lemon Trees

*after Eugenio Montale*

Listen:
the poets laureate live in a world
of plants whose names we're not likely to say.
But the roads I love
lead to weed-thronged gullies where a boy
can catch an eel sometimes
in a shrinking puddle:
narrow paths that wind around the hills,
drop through clumps of cattails
and enter an orchard, the rows of lemon trees.

It's best when even bird-song
evaporates into the blue sky:
then we can hear the friendly boughs
whisper in air that's just stirring
and we catch
the thick earth odor
that can pour an unsettling sweetness through us.
This is where all the passions fighting each other
miraculously stop:
this is where everyone's allowed a share of riches—
the fragrance of the lemon trees.

Look:
in these silences in which everything
loosens its hold on itself and seems
about to betray its last secret
we're almost sure
we're going to discover some flaw in nature—
the world's dead point, the weak link that gives,
the unraveling thread that finally leads us
into the presence of what is really true.
Carefully I look around,
my mind is trying all the possibilities,
it holds them one by one and then breaks them
in the thickening lemon-scent
as the late slow day begins to die.
These are the silences when
every retreating man-shadow
can look like the figure of some god who's lost his way.

That momentary illusion doesn't last, though—
time turns us back
to our clamoring cities where the blue gleams
only in high patches, between roof peaks.
The rain pools in the tired streets, a winter tedium
lies heavily on all the houses,
the light won't give us enough of itself, our souls grow bitter.
Yet one day through a gate that someone has left half open
there are yellow lemons shining at us
and our heart's ice melts
and into our empty being
again these golden horns of sunlight
can pour their songs.

# *Stars*

Her head bowed, the mother is silent now,
weak, with tears on her face; the father's
too weary to push his voice at the boy
any longer, and out of reasons why he should.

The boy, chin pointed at them both,
backs away another step, one hand behind him
reaching for the door he will close on them.
Everything is slowing now, running out, wearing down.

On the table the tepid food lies abandoned.
A cold breath across vast space goes
between them in this silence, and away
from each other they whirl in gigantic arcs.

# *Lovers*

Here is how it can be between a man and a woman:

In this handkerchief of his are tears he cried today—
    over her, for her, he doesn't know why he cried—
when she smiled a little, when he saw her
    recover, a little, from her fragility,
when he thought how much he loved her;
    how desperately he hoped she would be happy.

Once, she gave him a handkerchief of hers, perfumed
    in the instant when, standing before him alone
she pushed it down into her panties and pressed it
    against herself and brought it out again
still neatly folded, and smiling she gave it to him
    to carry with him on his journey.

    Mischief, happiness, sorrow, desire.

# *Hark*

Stars in the clear night sky more silent than any other silence,
even a cave's; and yet at each star the noise of fusion
blasts to beggar rockets massed in the millions, a roaring
multiplied to futile infinity out there, in the silent sky
over us, as we lie close listening to each other breathe,
hearing each other's heartbeats, sensing the smallest
candle wick of each other's noiseless warming desire.

# Analytical Episodes

First, how I loved
your life of feeling—unstinting
replenishings
for my miniature heart, that grew

.

But everything
hurts; our own wounded consciences
won't let us be—
we hear cries next door, and we cry

.

In daydreams, what
I see and want—the still aura
of if only
good things could stay so forever
(Old clothes on a hook, an open summer window)

.

Good news chastens;
I try not to hope—what happens
blows like pale straw
in the arriving winds, past us
(I will hold the moment's happiness)

.

Bad news shatters;
your soul is like a lovely vase
beautiful whole
dangerous and sharp in fragments
(I will gather them for you in my hands)

# *Poem*

Early on, uncertain, when we had
those few stolen clouded days along
a cold shore, in a gloomy house
an angle of sunlight shone in
for a moment through the windows and warmed us.

But with you for our secret while
that afternoon I lost my voice; I was
bewildered by you, made other by you,
and couldn't make, for that hour,
any sound at all, much less speak.

Now it seems to me I had to change
to become who I needed to be to be with you.
Now it seems to me that I needed to begin
over again from a time before I could speak.
Now it seems to me it was also through you
that then words came back to me.
Maybe it was so I could love you.
Maybe it was so I could say to you that I love you.
Maybe it was so I could say what I meant, to anyone.

two

# From a Paper Boat

*White gulls are brightest against the green river.*
*Flowers quicken, their hues flame, against the blue hill.*
*Just when I look, spring is over, once more.*
*When, on what day, will I be able to go home?*

—Tu Fu

The Emperor awarded me a year's living.
I spent the first two months in a mountain temple.
The blue trees at dusk were full of crows.
Then in the early spring I traveled to visit friends.

At night cold mists would gather, covering the stars.
To most of my friends life seemed endless war.
No one desired leisure for thought, but only to keep busy.
It snowed a little each night, and each day the sun melted the
    snow.

.

I had wished to spend time thinking and observing alone.
Departing without fanfare, as if again on the Emperor's business,
I had chosen to leave behind all responsibilities.
But soon I missed my family and decided I would return to them.

Then came the night of calamity darker than ten thousand nights.
Events cut me off, and when finally I reached our city
It had been destroyed, and with it all traces of my heart's care.
I repaired a small abandoned boat, and set out on the river.

.

Slowly I drifted away from our city, it did not matter to me
  where.
The riverbanks were scorched, and beyond them on both sides
Lay buildings blown down in the ashen streets.
I saw one burnt uncanny hand sticking up
Stiffly from a mere shadow, and remains
Of houses, crushed and tilted and collapsed
As if they had been no more than folded paper.

> .

In my wandering, after all whom I had loved
Were lost, at first I chose familiar harbors
So as to see the friends of my earlier years
From whose warm houses my itinerant service

Had always returned me to my own house, in time.
After mooring with haste to a quay of stone
I would leave my boat with quickened step
To find the streets and friends I remembered.

We would drink wine and talk all night long.
But now I tie up carefully and stay ashore only a short time.
I do not wish to see anyone I know. I buy my provisions,
I draw clean water from the town fountain, I return to my boat
  alone.

We used to sit outside among orange blossoms and jasmine
In the candlelit dark. But our talk made me feel unclean:
Each of us with his own complaint, mine not always the worst;
Or recounting, sometimes beautifully, the stories of victims.

> .

Several times, in my years of service, I had had to move my
family.
Mostly we lived far from the capital cities, in smaller towns.
Each day I was happy to return home from the fruitlessness of
offices.
When I saw my wife come out to meet me, crossing the muddy
cobbles,
Her every step endeared her to me.

Three times she made another being out of herself.
Once she wept over a dead child, no larger than her own hand.
Twice, with the blessings of gods and spirits, she gave birth to a
son.
She was more precious to me than all the Emperor's jade.
Yet when my year of leisure was awarded to me, I chose to travel
away.

.

The villages along the riverbank, for all their differences,
Their raids and rivalries, will always lie under the same stars;
And despite the changes in me and in this river,
When I lie on my back at night and look up
My memories are the same, they can see me no matter where I
go.

.

I remember the night when, in the small hours,
Having eluded muggers on the train platforms
And along the dark lengths of city blocks,
I returned home in the deep shadows.

After treading quietly up the steps of my porch
At the door I hesitated with my key.
My family was asleep inside, safely sheltered.
But I had brought with me the echoes of danger.

.

Once I heard someone say angrily behind me "Hurry up!"
When I turned I saw middle-aged men and women crossing the
    street.
They had fat cheeks, small eyes, open mouths, a slow gait.
They were held back in dulled childhood by the accidents they
    had inherited.
I went home early and my sons came running to greet me.

.

When we lived in the north, my wife and I rose early in summer.
We took our tea out to our back step, and sat down there.
Over us and our small house stood a huge willow tree.
Filled with a choir of birds, it seemed a protecting spirit.
She sat with her back straight, and looked into my eyes.

Then in under-a-blanket weather when horses ran at dawn
And at night the clear sky strewed galactic lilies
Far beyond and above the rushing of the cold earthly wind,
Inside and in silence we drank tea together by the fire,
Our heads close, knowing each other's thoughts.

.

Columns of boy conscripts still move over the roads.
Sometimes I have had to float past their riverbank camps at night,
With rags wrapped around my oar, to avoid their questions and
    threat.
They are always wearing new uniforms and boots,
And carrying new guns, new radios, new missiles, old swords.


                    ·


I wonder what our sons would have remembered of their
    childhood.
I recall what I would wish to forget.
There is almost nothing that does not come back to me.
Memory strikes my legs and gives me an idiot's gait of grief.
Any child's presence returns me to my longing for my own.


                    ·


I remember walking on Washington St. in my native city.
I heard "Shut up!" I turned and saw a sobbing three-year-old
Being hauled down the sidewalk by one arm, too fast.
I thought of taking ripe plums from a tree, and finding them
    bitter.


                    ·


That my sons would marry some day made me study young
    women.
I saw that some put themselves frighteningly at mercy:
In any cafe or gathering, the one whose lips held a cigarette
That a man's bullwhip would flick out; and the one
Around whom a knife-thrower was carefully patterning his
    daggers;

The one thrown repeatedly into the air who kept turning
Graceful somersaults as she fell back; and the one
Lifted in the lead elephant's mouth. To all these,
The great crowd roared its happiness at seeing them so
    endangered.

.

I was in the aisle of a supermarket one afternoon.
I heard behind me, "Put that back! Stop, damn it!"
I did not turn—I heard a smack, and the sort of small crying
That is already guarded, holding itself in.

.

That memorable night when I returned home late, I hesitated.
I stood in front of my door chasing a thought I never caught.
Finally I put my key in the lock, and went in.
After I had shut the door behind me, I stood alone.

Only one lamp was burning in the quiet house.
I said, Hurry up! Shut up! Stop, damn it! to the floor, to myself.
It was to test the power of demons that I spoke those things.
But that night my family was asleep and safe.

.

I have breathed again the scent of my children's rumpled beds.
I have received a hundred times the fateful letter from the
    Emperor.
Ten thousand times I have missed my chance to look into my
    wife's eyes
With thankfulness to her before we were never to see each other
    again.

.

Like stars in a small constellation that follow a brighter star,
Like a string of skiffs tied behind a slow-sailing ship,
Like cribs in a row down an orphanage ward,
Like goslings in a line behind a goose,
A file of small children walking along, I remember.

They were beside the green lawn of a saint's church, making no
    sound,
Each one reaching forward and back to hold the hands of others.
I thought they had been inside to see the mythical frescoes.
But they were led strictly by a nun, they were all blind.
They were out for the air, for the movement of their hesitant legs.


                    .


In the headlights of my stopped car on an empty country road,
My two small sons were chattering to each other, their hands
    darting.
It was after heavy rain, when the ditches were roaring.

Another car might come along, and I called to them.
Ten thousand new frogs no bigger than little grapes
Were hopping in the road, and my boys wanted to save them.


                    .


In a seaside town all of one color stone it was torrid summer.
For a week my wife and I rented a bedroom whose rightful
    tenant,
A widow, moved into her kitchen for the money we paid her.
In the morning we swam, in the afternoon we returned to the
    town.

Inside the hot shuttered bedroom we made love. Then we slept,
Breathing the sea-washed scent of our arms, our tangled legs.
When we woke it was cool again and we went out, looking at
     each other.
We walked along the top of the high town walls, beside the sea.

.

I am told of armies of orphan soldiers marching and destroying.
Once I saw a band of ragged boys that might have been them.
They walked slowly in the heat, laden with dusty weapons.
One of them led a young woman by a rope tied around her neck.

Sometimes, visiting an old friend, surprising him
With my coming unannounced when he had thought me dead,
I was greeted with happiness and a few oranges.
Then I heard of what one army or the other had done.

.

Many women admire the male strength that is not used
Against them. Or rather, when the male strength
Is restrained, holding its own arms back, force acting
With a volunteered tenderness, then many women admire it.

.

I have often seen young girls playing,
Unaware of what adults knew. They gambol through
The shopping malls and city streets pulling at
Their tired silent fathers who come bored and afraid
And angry from work in factories and mines.

If it were a daughter of my own listening to me
I would not want her to hear of what I have seen.
But when telling, why do I wish to tell
Of the end of hope, of the prison of what is?
If I make believe these words are mine, are they mine?

·

When I watched my sons play, I always hoped
That there was neither evil of which I did not know
Already stalking them, nor any suffering
Nor any distortion of their small being, that I myself
Might inflict on them. I wanted to hide them away,
As if they had been gold coins never to be spent.

I did not want their lives to fail of my witness.
As soon as I was apart from my sons, even for an hour,
I felt a terrible urgency to hurry back to them.
I was afraid for their safety. I could scarcely think.
Yet, even loving them as I did, when they were around me
I might chase them off so that I could continue my thinking in
    peace.

·

As a child, my wife was scarcely noticed.
Her father was an important man; her mother followed his
    wants.
I never remembered my own childhood very clearly.
My wife said it had fallen into a chasm of shadow
So that I might not suffer from having to see it again.

·

When our children were small, at night my wife's legs ached.
From standing and bending and carrying, she suffered pain.
I would invite her to sit calmly, take out her hairpins, rest.

I massaged the graceful length of her legs.
I brought a bowl of warm water for her sacred feet.
I washed them and rubbed warmth into her papery skin.

Thus also I cleansed my stale soul, my hands, of tobacco and ink.
I hoped then, I hope now, she did not dislike me.
From her came the scent of vanilla and scalded milk, of patience.

.

Sometimes I tie up beside a noisy riverman's hut full of life.
When a large boat passes, its wake reaches to each shore.
The wake does not move the hut or the banks of the river,
But it beats against my skiff, rocking me in it.

After the riverman's family is asleep,
The moon silvers the rippling wake of each night-sailing boat.
From on board, the sound of a man and woman talking
Will travel across the water, unknown to them.

It seems to me then that they are in life and I am no longer.
I grow older but I can grow no older.
They are traveling toward life, they look ahead to glimpse
And guess at it. I see it clearly, receding behind me.

.

In almost every man and woman I have met, I mark the child—
In the demeanor and gestures, in the way of smiling and of
    weeping,
In the casual greeting, whether it is open or guarded,
In the manner of defeat and in the moment of contentment.
Do others mark a child in me?
Is it too late to welcome the boy within the stringent man?
Is it too late to give refuge to the girl within the mirrored
    woman?
The wars of childhood come to an end,
But everyone who survives remains a refugee.


     .


Students stood thick in the square like grain before harvest.
After childhood, before manhood, there is a time
Of being only half in life. The other half
Stands not in death but in illusion and courage.
The full moon was following a red star
Through the sky each night, unable to catch it.

I was there, in the capital city. My boat was hidden
Under a ruined bridge where no lost people slept.
At one end of the huge square soldiers shouted
Through trumpets and raised a huge flag.
At the other, defiant students in their faded caps
Stood thick as the grain before the harvest.


     .


Now is a time of endings—of the year, the decade, the century.
Now opposites will struggle with more ferocity.
At night a gull looks black; the river is falling.
After midnight I am often startled by sirens and gunshots.

I lie awake in my boat, looking up and listening.
The Milky Way glows like spilled jewels too numerous to be
    gathered again.
From ten thousand houses I hear crying and shouts of despair.
Softer, some nights, there is laughter and a little singing.

Sometimes I can return to sleep. Sometimes I light
A candle and take out paper. I dip my brush in ink
And write out poems that I remember. Lines written down
In solitude survive, and I am in them as I write them.

·

All day geese cross the autumn sky, calling to each other.
Then a yellow moon rises, huge beyond masts and rooftops.
Late in the night, I hear more geese overhead.
Their voices come down as if from another time.

The limbs of my children were delicate, their speaking precise.
In autumn I sat one night under the sky listening for geese.
I remember my older son coming up behind me, I heard him
    approach,
He put his small hand on my shoulder and said, "Papa?"

My heart lies nearly still inside my ribs.
I remember his voice and that touch, and his childish
    handwriting.
I cannot think why I should breathe
Unless it were to hear the geese once more.

·

Yet it must be love, and even the memory of love,
Which, like clear water from a blue pitcher,
Spills over one's naked shoulders and hips
And rinses grief from the body,
Splashing it to the thirsty ground.


.


But my river has arrived at a place of sand where it is swallowed
    up.
I must walk across mountains and a dry plain.
Walking is a different rhythm from rowing or tending my sail:
My thoughts will wander with me in a different way.

I will keep my provisions, my brush and inkstone in a doll's
    house.
I will carry the doll's house on my back till I reach water again.
I will step out of my boat and turn and pick it up, too,
Carefully I will fold it and put it into my pocket.

I look back. Bright gulls are whitest against the river's green.
Against the blue hill flowers flame, their hues quicken.
Just when I look, spring is over, again.
On what day will I be able to go home? When?

three

# Piano (and Voice)

It answers or dins or touches gently or questions
but it cannot produce rising intensity in a single note or chord,
it cannot gasp or laugh or make any sound of breath,
which is why—with its own
percussive blows and arpeggiated caresses,
counterpoint and resolutions, myriad and melodic line,
behind and underneath and beyond
the singer's voice—
it becomes all the world that surrounds
a single person, the noise and silence both,
against which we speak or cry and with which
sometimes we find ourselves, for a little while,
in the music
of all the movement and some of the stillness
that we part to each side
as we go:
this king, some call it, of instruments
though I would rather say of its waiting keys:
the multitude, the many that accompany each one.

# An Explosion

It isn't the way it was
when he had strong legs,
thick arms, a handsome
wide back, and, in his house
clothes—rolled-up shirt
sleeves and a soft baggy
pair of pants that he especially
enjoyed putting on
after bathing—he would roam out
exhausted and loose-limbed
calling the three small boys
in for supper, and laughing
would gather them all at one time
and hold them hard against
his veiny body till they squirmed
and in that way he worked free
of his long shift in the pit.
At such moments he was kinder
than he was, and his wife, alive
and young then, seeing him
with his sons, could not but excuse
his other moments, and allow him
and everyone their choices,

although she would not
forgive the eternal owners
of the hollow hill.

He would trade the scrap of life
that he still has, but where
is the taker? His thin arms hang
and his neck's frail, his step's
cautious, he's cold, he coughs
and stands with others among whom
no one happens to know him
anymore near the mouth of the mine.

Several souls silently
rocket up unnoticed by anyone,
launched from inside the earth
and spinning like starfish thrown
as far out into the deep
earth's shadow as any
god's arm could fling them.

And a camera crew pushes hot
repelling lights and a mike
at the old man's face, which says,
"I've been waiting all night
now for my babes, I'm
hoping that they are alive."

# *Retributions*

**E**x farm boy hobbyist with horses, keeping one or two
not used for anything but his children's occasional riding,

my father had been waiting for this sign of luck
through years of his one good mare's many foalings

till it came on a brisk early morning with the newest colt,
that steamed where it had fallen out of her.

Into the sight of it we were initiated by stages—called from our
  beds
by mother, dressing quickly, then passed on to father

beyond the back yard fence: it wobbled up onto its legs and it had
the perfect markings, brown spots dappling its white rump.

Behind the corral built of scavenged planks my father
was burying the afterbirth he didn't want us to see.

Because we were children, we dreamed that this long-legged
colt might race someday, and we wondered if we'd ride it.

When it was two years old, no one having bothered even
to halter-break it worth a damn, it starved to death

in the neglected stable of the ambitious, profligate cousin
to whom my father, never a dime ahead, had felt

he'd had to sell it—albeit proudly, even hopefully, I'd guess.
Then twenty years later, when this cousin stopped

in a highway rainstorm to see if he could help a man
whose horse trailer had gotten stuck on the muddy shoulder

he was hit by a bus, injured and stupefied for life.
It may be everything is a coincidence with something else

and we don't notice the other half. It may be that only I
thought of the wasted colt of promise when I learned of the
    accident.

Anyway, now the memory of it newborn, my taciturn father's
    pride,
is just a dried stem and leaves that—when I think about my
    cousin

after having seen him sitting forever dazed, holding a cane—
that I discover by chance in the dictionary of feelings.

And although I had saved it this long, having put it
for safe keeping between pages of that most precious book,

I pick up that stem now and toss it away, and blow
the brittle leaves out after it and gone.

And that's how some rancorous deed of my own,
by me forgotten but linked to some other moment

by coincidences I never even knew, will be thrown at last
from someone else's on-moving life that somehow I damaged

when under blows I complete the pattern, I stagger
today or tomorrow: justice hard, deserved, unwitting.

# Order of Battle

[ 1 ]

The private corpse was rotting in the ditch
like good fruit ripped from a branch and thrown away,
proof that gain and loss of ground was crazy,
your life was nothing, it didn't matter much.

The bare gone flesh, the face a shape of slime,
the muddy bug-hole where the sex had been,
had no human look; and the tired platoon
stood near, no present danger, killing time.

Six days before, what happened happened quick,
four men lost at once, and Mitchell's balls.
They'd humped just far enough into the hills
to be too far from help, and here was payback.

When they first got out they'd made a count,
lied, called a dozen of the enemy dead,
but three of their own were missing, and they turned
around to get them, reinforced. Were sent.

They've found this one, the size of a naked boy,
that's all, could be Bernard or that skinny kid
nobody could count on, who never should
have been where he was needed, name of Jay.

[ 2 ]

Smoke so thick you couldn't see, and noise,
small arms coming in on every side,
the jungle vomiting, splitting open, fried,
freaking, sucking, or was that scream from us?

The LT'd stood up and cried and prayed to Hell
for a dustoff, his burnt arms raised, his legs
straddling Mitch, a stupid way to beg
for what's not coming, but he lived to tell

and Mitch will too but he would rather not.
The copter came and we were lifted out.
Every man running with a smoking butt
but those we didn't save, dead or hit.

[ 3 ]

My son, on a Saturday, comes in where I'll
be sitting, doing nothing, and he'll say,
"Dad, you want to watch the game with me?"
and I don't speak, he'll leave after a while.

No matter what they say or how they knew,
who could ever tell you what he saw—
the wet burnt flesh, the moment just before—
even if they told you ten times through.

You want to know what happened? Want me to say?
Want to hear me tell it, or maybe Mitch,
or who? You'll trade a drink? A cunt? A crutch?
Oh man.
　　　　Try this: it was a sunny day,

the sky was blue, the world was far away.
You were alone, you hoped and prayed they'd gone
and you'd never see them again, and what you'd done
and where you were was safe.
　　　　　　　　It wasn't.
　　　　　　　　　OK?


　　　　*Chi poria mai pur con parole sciolte*
　　　　*dicer del sangue e de la piaghe a pieno*
　　　　*ch'i' ora vidi, per narrar più volte?*

　　　　　　Inferno, XXVIII. 1–3

# César Vallejo's Heralds

Life deals such hard blows. . . I don't know.
Blows that might have come from the hatred of God Himself.
As if, in fright, the surge of everything suffered
sank back swirling into the soul. . . I don't know.

Not so many come; but come they do. . . They crack open
the fiercest countenance and wrack the strongest shoulders.
It may be they're the wild horses of some inhuman Attilas
or heralds in black sent toward us by Death.

They are the long plunge of the Christs of the soul
down from some holy faith that fate has already blasphemed.
Bloody blows, they're the crackling at the oven door
of some loaf of bread that's about to burst into flame.

And man. . . poor miserable creature. He turns his eyes
the way we do when someone claps us on the back,
he turns his frightened eyes, and everything he's lived through
sinks back down like a stagnant puddle of guilt in his glance.

Life deals such hard blows. . . I don't know.

# Madrid

Through stone portals and under colonnades
into the old central plaza in cold December
came gypsies and outcasts with green branches.

They had broken off whatever pines and spruce
had stood close along their routes to the city.
They had stripped copses and groves and plantations.

They camped on the cobbles, they lived in tents and wagons.
They sold the branches and a few small trees; some begged.
Little fires flickered in their artificial forest.

They seemed to have brought with them into the plaza
the stillness they had torn out of the woods,
as if to sustain the peace that the city would tear out of them.

Overheard, their voices sounded raw and smoky, as if used up.
But late, rising above the noise of cars and of children
playing at all hours, there might be a guitar and singing.

Catching my coat sleeve, their beautiful dirty children
improvised intricacies of delay, so as to praise and hawk
the scent of green, so as to implore and beguile.

I was outside their thoughts, I was outside their ways.
We judged each other, I bought their wasted pine boughs.
Their children stole my coin, I stole their image.
Now we are all outside that time, we are all inside this language.

# Hide from Time

I was about to return to our Sunday,
love, to the two of you, but a sliver of winter
sunlight lay on the stair like a feather.

Rather than mountains or any beautiful
views of mountains, rather than rivers
down which I could float my gaze,

I'd want this stray feather on the stairs
up to our room and our daughter's room
far from airplanes and faraway hurricanes

of night-fears and the daily inevitable
beginnings of the workdays schooldays
when she leaves and I leave and you leave

pulling threads of each other with us
through the hours while the luckless must seek
shelter and warmth and the loveless

must hope and connive and believers
must pray and depressives must live
their un-life unwillingly,

and we hope we won't, our daughter will never,
be one of those, at the mercy of others, of all
that changes, of hard everything, iron and ironic.

This isn't a feather I can pick up.
It's starting to fade—a cloud or the movement
in one minute of the earth. *Are you coming?*

you call to me. This universe is still creating itself
and like all mere matter maybe we come from
four billion years ago till we three

spin into being and braid our courses.
From the decks of ships I've seen what infinity
looks like in the night sky, it pulls vision

away, far past the intervening mist
of stars, until for all their known size
they seem only trembling microbes of light

in the biggest dish, and as if we've been
tossed up by a wave from the incalculably
slow churning, microbes on a microbe,

electrons on an atom of an atom,
we float in mid-cosmos,
life an instant, before we fall back

alongside but faster than
flensed planets and ipsitive suns,
all the most and least promising things.

Now I'm going, too. I call, *I'm coming.*
The feather's gone and you're waiting.
Both of you, I love.

# Question

Today? Tomorrow?
Why was he given
this happiness? Did
he ask for it in
his weakest moments?
Yes, he pleaded for
it. But did there have
to be for even
those few moments a
God who could give him
this? He hadn't thought
so but if there was
It was only strong
enough to give him
this happiness and
then leave him with no
power to keep it.
So it's going to
be taken from him,
so he'll be kicked like
a dog, crushed like a
mouse, tormented like
a bug, treated in

other words like a
human being. When?
Tomorrow? Today?

# Atlantic Incident

I'd pictured floating matterhorns.
I'd have expected crashing falls of ice
from them as they drifted south
into the shipping lanes
after they'd broken off of vast floes
at the end of summer
and begun to crack and melt.

But I noticed the Turkish bo's'n—
who alone among the caterwauling
Christian crew was sober—
looking down from the end of the wing
of the bridge in the moonlight,
intent on some big chunks
that only he had noticed
riding low in the troughs,
as fog was thickening.

The freighter slowed, the officers
came out of their cabins buttoning up
and sent a groggy sailor forward
to lean out over the prow
holding a walkie-talkie

so he could warn of what might slice
a gash in the hull or bash entirely
through it, although avoiding the blow
even with a quick rudder seemed unlikely.
After midnight, when here and there
the fog-diffused moonlight
was making them glow like phosphorescent bathtubs,
I went to bed—to sleep
or drown, as the icebergs determined.

The sea was open again in the early morning,
the air clear, the ship back up to speed.
At breakfast the captain and first mate,
their eyes bloodshot, the uniforms
they had dozed in by turns very rumpled,
were drinking black coffee and eating
privileged portions of eggs and meat.
How many were there? I asked.
Vee shtopped gounting after two hundert,
the captain said, without looking up
from his plate. He reached for the salt
and asked the first mate, Vould you say a tousant?
The man was spearing a peeled, gleaming potato
and answered softly, "Ja."

# From an Early Train
# in Spring

**T**he sun rose on all river-life—

Sun on Red Wing Malting Co, sun on Kish Electric, sun on Farmers Coop and Supply, sun on Simak's Meats-Seafood, sun on Wilkie Insurance, sun on fumes rising above the refinery towers, sun breaking some of those poisons down and burning others to greater virulence.

Sun on silos both trim and weathered, both full and empty, sun on fields just planted, on damp roads, on a yellow willow.

Sun on small islands, on lilacs leaking a purple scent, on scrub and weed and rock.

Sun warming Jerseys and Guernseys, sun on the stone foundations of barns, on the walls and the roofs, on farmhouses and sheds.

Sun on ditched cars and junked stoves, sun piercing gullies and underbrush, greening new leaves and bleaching dead limbs.

Sun on depots and sidings.

Sun on driftwood and wavelets, on a fisherman standing knee-deep in a seething glitter.

Sun on a red pickup racing this train.

Sun on a lost penny, somewhere.

Sun on coal and gravel in river barges.

Sun on dandelions and daisies and cattails and clover.

Sun on the sumac choking riverbank and slopes.

Sun on tanks of Industrial Molasses, on heaps of old tires and scrap metal, on the rusting wreck of Sanjay's Super Rocket parked for the last time at the back of a junkyard.

Sun on a great blue heron stalking still shallows, sun on a multitude of unmoving turtles.

Sun on poor Ned, waking wrapped in cardboard on the ground behind Anson Bros. Grain, sun on his pale eyes, who looks up and shifts to get more of the warmth, and says, Jesus this is some sunshine this morning.

# Teacher

Stillness and silence deepen in the last light.

Across the glossy luminous water a muskrat
noses a passage, trailing a clean wake.
Nearer, circles ripple outward where a fish
came up with open jaws on a mayfly.

The fire crumbles down, crackling.
Near the canoe, the washed skillet and plates
drip upside down onto a cold rock-shelf.

The wind begins to breathe and blow
through the spruce-tops, they creak and the food duffel
sways where we hung it, up in the branches, high.

At this little lake, this floor
of one shaft of heaven, the peppermint
we trampled when we were hammering stakes
scents our darkness inside the tent;
mosquitoes patter against the nylon like rain.

We shift and settle our hips and shoulders
till they'll accept their own weight. It's only
a little, what we know or hope to know.

The loons seem to break their laughter with a cry.

# Prospect of a Village in Devon

## [ 1 ]

It was steep walking up
past green fields neatly bounded
to the high crossing of narrow hedged lanes
behind the village where one winter we lived.
Fast gray clouds would scud
across the sky in waves from the west,
stripes of a clean blue in the gaps between them.
The lane sides were like ruins of walls,
layers of rocks and tangled root,
stiff gorse beginning to brighten
with yellow blooms,
an elm every so often or the stump of one
diseased and cut down;
and quiet, peace, the great sky.
Near the summit, when brief spring sunlight
struck some bare poplars, starlings there
would begin to sputter and pipe,
their hollow throats throbbing
as they bobbed on twigs
by a sheltered barn beneath the crest.
Cloud-shadow would quieten them again.

## [ 2 ]

The several of us
strung along the climb
were all warmed by the walking
that made the body of the landscape
breathe with our stride.
Below us mapping its own way
was the River Exe, mild
between grassy banks—looking
like hammered silver chain as the pale
cloud-light and sunshine took turns
dulling and sparkling its curves through pastures.
And the ancient boundary ditches that webbed
the hill contours are all paved lanes now—
anyone could see how to our village
they ran up along paths of retreat,
anyone could hear how
carried inside the meaningless sound of the wind
was always another sound, that could be,
for its plaintiveness, a plea.

## [ 3 ]

A low-whistling wind with a claw in it
had been dragging and tearing the topmost trees,
winter and summer, for longer than measured time.
Sheltered from it by the remnant of a stone wall
I pondered what thoughts came to mind:
It was a beautiful view
that deserted summit gave—
nearby farmsteads, our village atop a lower hill,
another village beyond the river,
and hedges and more farmsteads and fields.

Faithfully the scene
was always waiting for anyone
who needed the sight of this one small
particularly neat county of man
to walk up to get it, and watch
the consoling movement of cloud
shadows across silent fields that can't
feel their touch, or return it.
Up there, there was nothing to say;
there was only the shared hour spent
above a scarred world
that from the height looked safe
as far as we could see.

[4]

But bitter winter
tasting of tarnished steel
had visited and can return.
Who pleads with the wind?
Is it in answer to any voice
that it will break from time to time
or let smoke rise a little straighter?

Should I echo cries that once
we might have heard from here,
as when into local fields like all these
fell the extra bombs
dropped to lighten fleeing planes?
Or did cries and alarms come this far
even from the burning city?
Or, beyond it, from the hidden chimneys
of the place those planes came from?
From what place, however cold and low,
can a yellow star not be seen?

## [ 5 ]

Over the low roaring of the wind in the shell
of my ear I heard one distant car that day,
returning perhaps from an innocent errand
in the town, and then
I spied the dull roof of it,
tiny and toiling up the trench
of the narrow road between hedges
toward a hilltop along the route of all
the events this landscape holds—
like an idea,
a solution, traveling at last
to the top of the head:
and I wondered how to speak it.

## [ 6 ]

And the ragged starlings in the naked trees
begin to squawk some raucous praise,
it must be, of the rising, ready,
open, storied moment
that lies in view—
praise of courage and pity,
and still the call
for a different story
everywhere under the sun.